THE SHINING OF BEING

THE ESSENCE OF MEDITATION SERIES

THE SHINING

of

BEING

Rupert Spira

SAHAJA

SAHAJA PUBLICATIONS

First published in 2025 by Sahaja Publications
PO Box 887, Oxford OX1 9PR, United Kingdom
www.sahajapublications.com

Designed by Rob Bowden

ISBN 978-1-0686453-2-7

For my mother

CONTENTS

ACKNOWLEDGEMENTS

When I contemplate who I might thank for helping to elicit the understanding contained in this book, I am taken on an almost endless reverie into past and present friendships. I wish I could thank you all individually.

But I will name just a few. First, I would like to thank my dear mother, who passed away recently. I owe everything to her. When a friend asked me how I came by my great love of truth, I replied that my mother had introduced me to the non-dual understanding in my teenage years. He paused for a moment and then said, 'How beautiful! The mother handing her son back to God.' My mother did indeed hand me back to God, and I am eternally grateful to her.

Second, I would like to thank my companion, Kyra. Many years ago, she said to me, 'Teach me about God.' Little did I realise then, how much she would teach me about the divine.

I would like to thank my son, Matthew, whose sincerity, honesty and integrity are a constant inspiration to me.

I would like to thank all the attendees of my meetings and retreats. Your love of truth has drawn this understanding, such as it is, out of me. This book would not have happened without you.

Finally, I would like to thank Kyra for distilling the essence of numerous meditations into this manuscript; Joel Drazner and James Haig for preparing the text for publication; and Rob Bowden for designing the book. Each of you held a vision – to create a book that shines with being – and your thoughtfulness, sensitivity and intelligence have brought that vision into form. I'm deeply grateful.

Most people seek peace and happiness in objects, substances, activities and relationships. Sooner or later, these fail to deliver their promise of fulfilment, and many turn to a religious or spiritual tradition.

These traditions offer a wealth of approaches, which can be distilled into three categories: the Progressive Path, the Direct Path and the Pathless Path. There are numerous Progressive Paths; there is one Direct Path, and the Pathless Path cannot really be said to be a path.

The Progressive Path and Direct Path begin with the presumption of separation: the belief that each of us is a separate individual in a world of objects and others. Both these paths give the individual something to do: a method to practise, a path on which to progress and a goal to aim for.

The Progressive Path suggests directing our attention towards a single object of experience.* Instead of losing ourselves

---

* By *object of experience*, I refer not only to a physical object but to anything that is limited in time or space, such as a thought, feeling, sensation, perception, activity or relationship.

in thoughts, feelings, sensations, perceptions, activities, relationships and so on, we focus on *one* thing. It may be a physical object, such as a candle flame, or a subtle object, such as a mantra. In both cases, we are gathering and steadying the divergent energies of the mind onto a single object. For this reason, the various practices that compose the Progressive Path, from mindfulness to mantra meditation, could be called 'objective meditation'. That is, we progress to the peace of our true nature via an object of experience.

To understand how objective meditation works, it's helpful to understand the meaning of the word 'attention'. Attention is derived from the Latin prefix *ad*, meaning 'to' or 'towards', and *tendere*, meaning 'to stretch', implying that attention is the stretching or directing of awareness towards an object of experience.

In other words, we could say that awareness directed towards an object is attention, and attention divested of its object is awareness.

If attention could be likened to the beam of light emitted from a torch, then awareness would be the bulb. As such, attention is like a two-way street. It can be traced outwards towards its object or inwards towards its source. The source of attention is always the same: our true nature of being, being aware or awareness itself.* The object of attention could be any object of experience: a thought, feeling, sensation, perception and so on.

* I use the terms *being, being aware* and *awareness* synonymously.

Attention could also be likened to stretching a rubber band between two points: the source of attention (awareness) and its object (such as the words you are reading now). In the case of objective meditation, the object might be a mantra. Instead of allowing the mind to wander amongst numerous objects of experience, we steady the mind on a single point. This interrupts the mind's habitual engagement in the content of experience and prepares it for its subsidence into the heart of being.

How does this relaxation of the mind take place? Consider what happens to a stretched rubber band when one end is released. The rubber band springs back to its natural, relaxed condition. In the same way, as the mantra fades, the keen focus of attention relaxes and, as a result, attention subsides back into its source. It relaxes back into its natural condition of being, being aware or awareness itself, and tastes its true nature of peace.

*   *   *

The second approach, the Direct Path, is less common than the first. Instead of directing our attention towards an object of experience, we are encouraged to investigate the *subject* of experience, the source of attention. This could be called 'subjective meditation' or self-enquiry.

This approach is often initiated by a question: What is it that knows or is aware of our experience? What is it that remains consistently present throughout the three states of waking, dreaming and sleeping? To whom does my experience appear? Who am I really? A Zen koan would fit into this category, 'What is, but does not exist?' Such questions invite the mind backwards, inwards or 'self-wards', encouraging its subsidence into its source, the ground of being.

In this approach, we do not proceed to our true nature via an object of experience. We go directly from our current experience, irrespective of its content, to our true nature of being, being aware or awareness itself. We go directly to the source of attention without taking the intermediary step of focusing on an object. It is for this reason that this approach is sometimes referred to as the 'Direct Path'.

The Direct Path is sometimes described as the inversion or turning around of attention. Instead of focusing on an object, we turn our attention around and direct it back towards our self. While this is a legitimate way of speaking, it can be misleading. Just as a beam of light from a torch cannot be turned around and directed towards the bulb, so we cannot really attend to our self. That is, awareness cannot 'stretch itself' towards itself. It can only attend to something other than itself. So, it would be more accurate to describe self-enquiry as the relaxing or subsiding, rather than the focusing or directing, of attention.

The sun can shine its light on everything in the universe apart from itself. It can shine its light on the earth, for example, because the earth is at a distance from it. But it cannot shine its light on itself, because it is too close to itself.

However, the sun does not need to shine its light on itself. It illuminates itself just by being itself. In other words, the sun is self-luminous. Its nature is illumination. Shining is what the sun *is*, not what it does.

For the same reason, we – being, being aware or awareness itself – cannot attend to our self. We can only attend to something other than our self. Awareness can shine its light on an object of experience, but it cannot shine its light on itself. It is too close to itself. However, awareness does not need to shine its light on itself because its *nature* is being aware.

Just as the sun is self-luminous, so our being is self-knowing or self-aware. Just as the sun illuminates itself simply by being itself, so our being knows itself by being itself. It knows itself, or illuminates itself, just by being itself. It is, as such, self-luminous.

*   *   *

The third approach, the Pathless Path, is even less common than the Direct Path. Unlike the first two paths, it does not begin with the presumption of separation. It starts with the understanding that, at the deepest level, we already are pure being, being aware or awareness itself. As such, there is little need for elaboration. After all, being does not need to *be* told to be, let alone to practise being itself. Our true nature needs no spiritual instruction. On the Pathless Path, we start with our true nature and stay there.

The Progressive Path and Direct Path make numerous compassionate concessions to the separate self we seem to be. The Pathless Path makes few such concessions. It says, 'Simply being is your nature; abide as that'. In other words, don't mediate; just be. Simply being is the origin, the path and the goal.

On the Progressive Path and Direct Path, the separate self is what we *seem to be*, and meditation is what we *do*. On the Pathless Path, meditation is what we *are*, and the separate self is an activity that we *do*.

*   *   *

To summarise, the great religious and spiritual traditions can be distilled into three approaches, and each approach has a corresponding method or meditation practice. On the Progressive Path, we practise objective meditation. That is, we give our attention to an object of experience, such as a mantra or the breath. On the Direct Path, we practise subjective meditation. That is, we relax the focus of our attention from the known and explore the knower or the subject of experience. On the Pathless Path, we simply remain as being before it is coloured or qualified by the content of experience. It could, as such, be referred to as 'non-meditation'. This non-meditation, or simply being, is the essence of all experience and the subject of this book.

Simply being is the pinnacle of self-knowledge and the highest meditation. It is the meditation for which all other meditations are a preparation and into which they eventually resolve. Simply being is also the ultimate prayer and the consummate act of devotion.

Divested of the qualities that our being seems to derive from the content of experience, it stands revealed as infinite being, God's being, the only being there is.* In other words, in simply being, the separate self that we seem to be is utterly subsumed in God's infinite being.

Simply being is the culmination of all the great religious and spiritual traditions. It is the point at which the path of knowledge and the path of devotion merge. As the Sufis say, 'I searched for God and found only myself. I searched for myself and found only God.'

Simply being is what the Zen masters evoke when they say, 'Show me your original face before you were born.'† It is what Jesus referred to when he said, 'Before Abraham was, I am.'‡ It is what the Buddha evoked in his wordless Flower Sermon, in which he simply held up a flower. All teachings, pathways and practices evolve from, and eventually converge in, simply being.

To abide as that is the essence of meditation and the heart of prayer.

---

* *God* refers to ultimate reality, or that which truly is – infinite, eternal, self-aware being. Thus, *God* and *being* are used synonymously.
† This quote is associated with Case 23 of the 13th-century Zen koan collection, Mumonkan, or 'Gateless Gate'.
‡ John 8:59

CHAPTER I

THE EXPERIENCE OF BEING

He who looks outside, dreams;
he who looks inside, awakes.
CARL JUNG

What is the very first thing we can say about ourself?

'I am.'

From what experience is the statement 'I am' derived?

The statement 'I am' is derived from the simple experience of being.

How can I say with certainty, 'I am'?

I can say 'I am' because I *know* that I am. I am *aware* that I am. I am aware of being. In other words, the statement 'I am' refers to the awareness of being.

And what is it that knows or is aware that I am?

I know that I am. *I* am aware that I am.

Is the 'I' that I *am* different from the 'I' that *knows* that I am, or is it the same 'I'?

Obviously, it is the *same* 'I'. The 'I' that I *am* and the 'I' that *knows* that I am are the *same* 'I', that is, the same being.

The being that I essentially am is aware of itself. Just as the sun is self-luminous, so being is self-aware.

*   *   *

The experience of being is our primary knowledge of ourself. It shines in the mind as the knowledge 'I am'.

It is more intimate and familiar to us than our most intimate thoughts, feelings and sensations – indeed, the experience of being is the most intimate, familiar experience there is.

All other knowledge about ourself takes place after the experience of being. For example, the knowledge 'I am' is *prior* to the knowledge 'I am sad', 'I am drinking tea', 'I am thirty-three years old' and so on. It is prior to the knowledge 'I am a man' or 'I am a woman' or even 'I am a human being'. It is always the same 'I am', which is temporarily qualified by a feeling, activity, age and so on.

The experience of being is prior to all other knowledge and experience. All other knowledge and experience is added to our being, just as a movie is added to the screen. For instance, in order to feel 'I am sad', the 'I am' must first be present. The feeling of sadness is added to the knowledge 'I am'. The feeling at some point disappears, but the 'I am' remains. Then, another experience arises, is added to the 'I am', temporarily qualifies it and then vanishes. But the 'I am' always remains. It is the transparent background that is consistently present throughout the drama of our lives.

Having said that, the phrase 'the experience of being' can be misleading. Being is not an object of experience like a thought, the taste of tea or the sensation of warmth on our skin. Being is what we essentially are. It is our essential, irreducible self. It can never be known as an object.

When the sun shines on the moon, the sun is the subject of the illumination, and the moon is the object. In other words, the illumination takes place in subject-object relationship. However, the sun's illumination of *itself* doesn't take place in subject-object relationship. The sun illuminates itself just by being itself.

Likewise, when we know an object of experience, we do so in subject-object relationship: 'I know a thought', 'I love you', 'I see a tree'. There is always a subject knowing, feeling or perceiving an object. However, when we know our *self* – that is, when our being knows itself – the self that knows and the self that is known are the *same*. In other words, the knowing of our own being does not take place in subject-object relationship. Our being knows itself simply by being itself.

*   *   *

Ask yourself, 'Am I having the experience of simply being?' That is, 'Can I say of my own experience, "I am"'? To answer the question, we pause, check our experience and then answer 'yes'.

What takes place in that pause? To what experience do we refer that enables us to answer 'yes' to the question, 'Am I having the experience of simply being?'

Imagine I were to ask you, 'Are you having the experience of thoughts?' You would pause and say 'yes'. In that pause, you would refer to your thoughts.

Imagine I were to ask you, 'Are you having the experience of the tingling sensation at the soles of your feet?' You would pause and say 'yes'. In that pause, you would refer to the tingling sensation at the soles of your feet.

Are you having the experience of simply being?

Pause.

'Yes.'

What happens in that pause?

You become aware of being.

In fact, you did not *become* aware of being. You are *always* aware of being. Or rather, being is always aware of itself.

To illustrate this, we can try a simple exercise. Become aware of your breathing.

You were probably not aware of your breathing before I made that suggestion. Perhaps your attention was absorbed in your thoughts, the words on this page or the sounds in your room. Of course, as soon as I suggested becoming aware of your breathing, you suddenly seemed to notice your breathing. In fact, you were experiencing your breathing all along. However, breathing is such a subtle experience compared with your thoughts, feelings and perceptions that it tends to recede into the background of experience. Therefore, it was only when I mentioned it that you seemed to notice it.

Our being is even subtler than the breath. It is the silent, empty background of all experience, just as the screen is the transparent background of all the colourful images in a movie. Just as we are always aware of our breath, so we are always aware of being, although it is usually obscured by the content of experience.

*   *   *

Let us consider another example. Imagine I were to suggest that you become aware of the space in the room in which you are currently sitting. You would soften the focus of your attention from the objects in the room and suddenly become aware of the space. In fact, you were always experiencing the space, but your experience of the space seemed to be obscured by your experience of the objects – the table, the chairs, the books and so on.

Even though we are experiencing space all the time, we don't notice it due to the exclusive focus of our attention on the contents of our room. In other words, even though we are always experiencing the space, we overlook it because it is empty and thus does not call for our attention.

Likewise, we tend to overlook our being precisely because it is so transparent and intimate. We fail to notice it due to the exclusive focus of our attention on the content of experience. It is pure peace and, therefore, does not call for our attention.

Compared with the transparency of being, the content of experience is so fascinating and colourful that we tend to lose ourself in it. Our attention becomes absorbed in thoughts, feelings, perceptions, activities and relationships at the expense of being. As our attention is drawn into the foreground of experience, being seems to recede into the background. As a result, we overlook our being in favour of the content of experience, just as we fail to notice the space in favour of the objects in the room.

For instance, when we are walking down the street, all the corresponding sensations and perceptions absorb our attention and, as a result, obscure the intimacy of simply being. When we say, 'I am anxious', 'I am tired' or 'I am sad', we acknowledge that the 'I am' is present in the experience, but the feeling of anxiety, tiredness or sadness veils it. The pure 'I am' is obscured by the colours of experience, and hence we lose touch with it. Being becomes so utterly intimately immersed in the content of experience that it overlooks itself, thereby losing touch with its innate peace.

* * *

In meditation or prayer, we disentangle ourself from the content of experience and come back to the simple fact of being. We come back to our self; we return to the sanctuary of being.

Our being is the place of peace within us. It is prior to and independent of the content of experience. Our being is ever-present, always available and always in the same pristine condition. It is our true home.

Simply being may not seem like much to the object-knowing mind, but it is actually the highest form of meditation and the ultimate prayer. It is, at once, the most profound knowledge and the greatest act of worship.

The essence of meditation or prayer is to abide in being, as being. It is the meditation for which all other meditations are a preparation. It is what the Christian mystic Meister Eckhart referred to when he said, 'When we come to the One that gathers all things up into itself, there we must stay.'*

When we come out of meditation – that is, when we cease resting in being, as being – and return to our everyday life, nothing happens to our essential self or being. Nothing happens to the 'I am'. It is just temporarily mixed with the contents of experience and seems to acquire their qualities, just as a screen is temporarily coloured by the drama in a movie and seems to assume its characteristics.

For instance, when we say, 'I am tired', 'I am lonely' or 'I am sad', the 'I am' is temporarily qualified by a feeling.

* My rendition from *Meister Eckhart*, translated by Raymond Bernard Blakney (Harper & Brothers, 1941).

When we say, 'I am twenty-six' or 'I am sixty-three', the same 'I am' is qualified by an age. When we say, 'I am single' or 'I am married', the same 'I am' is qualified by a relationship. When we say, 'I am reading a book' or 'I am drinking tea', the same 'I am' is qualified by an activity.

But in all these experiences – indeed, in *all* experience – nothing happens to the 'I am'. It always remains the same, like the screen.

Meditation or prayer is simply to remain as the 'I am', prior to and in the midst of all experience. As such, meditation or prayer has nothing to do with the content of experience. It is simply to recognise the intimate and ever-present experience of being, and to remain as that. Therefore, meditation is not something we 'do' with the mind. It is simply to be as we always and already are.

In everyday life, we emphasise experience at the expense of being. In meditation or prayer, we magnify being at the expense of experience. As such, meditation or prayer is simply the shining of being.

* * *

Our being is utterly intimate yet shares none of the qualities of our personal, finite experience. As such, it is impersonal and infinite.

Our being is like the space in a room. The space in a room is not really *in* the room; it is the vast, empty space of the universe. There isn't a different space for every bedroom, kitchen or office on the planet. There is *one* physical space in the universe that completely fills every room but is neither contained within nor limited by any particular room. The space is, as such, unlimited or infinite.

Likewise, just as the space fills a room but extends way beyond its four walls, our being pervades the body but extends beyond its limitations. The belief that our being is limited to, and shares the characteristics of, the body is like believing that the space in the room is limited. Just as we can understand that the space of a room does not share the limitations of the four walls of the room, we can see that our essential being does not share the limitations or characteristics of the body. Our body has a form and is limited, but our essential being is formless and without limit. Just as the space is not contained within the four walls of a room, so our being is not imprisoned in the body. It fills and pervades the body but extends beyond its limitations. This is why Rumi asked, 'Why stay in prison when the doors are wide open?' *

The apparently limited space of a room is a mixture of the unlimited space of the universe and the four walls of the room. Likewise, the separate self that we seem to be is a mixture of infinite being and the body.

As such, our being is not really *our* being. That is, it does not belong to our body. It is simply *being*, unlimited being. And how many unlimited beings can there be? How many

* *The Essential Rumi*, translated by Coleman Barks (HarperOne, 2004).

unlimited spaces in the universe are there? Just as there is only one physical space in the universe, so there is only one being. There is one intimate, infinite and indivisible being from which everyone and everything derive their apparently independent existence.

*   *   *

If this intimate, infinite and indivisible being were to give itself a name, it would call itself 'I', for 'I' is the name that that which knows itself gives to itself. As such, 'I' is infinite being's name for itself; it is the divine name. The mind should tremble at the name 'I'. It should stand before it as does a candle to the sun.

Meditation or prayer is to lose oneself so deeply in 'I' that it is divested of all the qualities that it derives from experience until it stands revealed as intimate, impersonal, infinite being. Meister Eckhart referred to this when he said, 'Since it is God's nature not to be *like* anyone, we have to come to the state of being *nothing* in order to enter into the same nature that He is.' *

Our primary knowledge of ourself is not 'I am a woman', 'I am a man' or even 'I am a person'. It is simply 'I am'. Our primary knowledge is not even that I am a *human* being, but that I am *being*. Even the knowledge 'I am a human being' is secondary to our knowledge of ourself as simply being.

---

* *The Complete Mystical Works of Meister Eckhart*, translated by Maurice O'C. Walshe (Herder & Herder, 2010).

We typically think that experiences such as sadness, tiredness or loneliness are temporary feelings that qualify us as human beings, but we can go a step further. Even the experience of being human is a temporary state of pure being. At the deepest level, we are not human beings; we are pure being, temporarily clothed in human experience.

It is this recognition, the recognition of the divine in us, that makes us truly humane. The qualities that are innate in being, such as peace, happiness and love, inspire actions in our lives such as creativity, kindness and compassion. These are expressions of the divine qualities in our everyday lives.

When we take the final step from knowing ourself as a human being to knowing ourself as simply being, we 'come to the state of being nothing', as Meister Eckhart said. In doing so, we are 'one with God's nature'.

In some mediaeval paintings, people are depicted with golden halos around their heads. This golden halo signifies the shining of being, the shining of God's presence in that person, as that person.

The Pathless Path is to be only that, to know only that and to love only that. We stand as infinite being and see only that in everyone and everything.

CHAPTER 2

THE WATER IN THE WINE

Just as every drop of the ocean carries the taste of the ocean,
so does every moment carry the taste of eternity.
SRI NISARGADATTA MAHARAJ

We are all experiencing our self all the time. That is, everyone always feels, 'I am myself'.

Imagine we were to ask anyone, 'Are you yourself?' They would answer, 'Yes'. Why? Because we are all having the experience of being our self, irrespective of whatever thoughts, feelings and perceptions may be present.

What is this essential experience of our self? The experience of our self is not the experience of a thought. It is not a feeling, a sensation or a perception. It is not an activity or relationship. It is just the experience of being.

Everyone is experiencing their self, their being, in all places and at all times without exception. Simply being is the most obvious, intimate and familiar experience there is. We refer to the fact of simply being when we say, 'I am'. At any moment of experience, we can all say with absolute certainty, 'I am'.

Not only do we experience our self all the time, we feel that we are essentially the same self throughout our entire lives. We feel that the self we are now is the same self we were this morning, ten months ago, ten years ago or when we were ten days old. Our bodies and minds have changed innumerable times over the years, but our essential self has remained the same.

The experience of being is a continuous thread that runs throughout our entire lives. In fact, it is the only continuous element of experience. The content of experience consists of thoughts, feelings, sensations and perceptions. None of these are continuous. They are all intermittent. They begin and end, but the 'I am' remains consistently present.

If our life were likened to a necklace, all our changing experiences would be the colourful beads, and the 'I am' would be the invisible thread on which they are strung. The beads are many and varied – thoughts, feelings, sensations, perceptions, activities, relationships and so on – but they are all strung on a single thread, 'I am'. Without the thread, there would be no necklace. The 'I am' is the thread that holds all experience together. It is the golden thread of being on which our colourful experiences are strung.

*   *   *

All experience consists of two elements: one, changeless and ever-present; the other, changing and temporal.

When we describe our self, we say, 'I am lonely', 'I am hungry' or 'I am reading a book'. It is always the same 'I am', qualified by a temporary feeling, sensation, activity and so on.

While the content of experience is always changing, the experience 'I am' remains the same. There is no break in the golden thread of 'I am'.

We start each sentence with 'I am' because our self lies at the heart of, and pervades, all experience. Our being is the changeless element in all changing experience.

Our feelings, sensations and activities are always changing. None of these experiences are essential to us. They are added to us and removed from us, but being shines throughout.

Just as none of the beads on the necklace are essential to it, so no experience is essential to our self. Experiences are like ornaments that decorate the 'I am' but are not essential to it. The beads can be removed, and the necklace remains as it is. Likewise, thoughts, feelings and perceptions can be removed from us, but our being remains as it is: pristine, ever-present, luminous, still and at peace.

* * *

If peace and happiness are the very nature of our being, and we are always experiencing our being, then why don't we experience peace and happiness all the time?

The reason is simple. Whilst we are always experiencing our being, we don't all experience our being clearly, as it essentially is. Our being is entangled with the content of our experience.

When we drink tea, coffee or wine, we are mostly drinking water. But we don't realise that we are drinking water as the water is mixed with various flavours, sweet or bitter.

It is the same with our self or being. In every experience we have, whether pleasant or unpleasant, we are experiencing our being. Being is shining clearly in the midst of each experience. However, our being merges with the flavours of experience.

Just as water that is infused with apples, grapes or tea seems to acquire their flavours, so our being, when mixed with the qualities of experience, seems to acquire their characteristics.

If water is mixed with chocolate, it tastes of chocolate. If water is mixed with tea, it tastes of tea. Likewise, if our being is mixed with the agitation of our thoughts, we feel, 'I am agitated'. The pure 'I am' becomes 'I am agitated'. If our being is mixed with sadness or loneliness, the pure 'I am' becomes 'I am sad' or 'I am lonely'.

In this way, our being is mixed with the content of experience and no longer 'tastes' itself as it truly is. That is, we become absorbed in the content of experience and, as a result, temporarily lose touch with our innate peace and quiet joy.

*   *   *

Meditation or prayer is to recognise the nature of our being before it is mixed with or qualified by experience, and simply to abide as that. It is to taste the water instead of tasting the wine. In all these drinks – tea, coffee, orange juice and so on – the water is the thirst-quenching element. Likewise, our essential being is the thirst-quenching element in all experience. That is, our being is the only element of experience that can truly satisfy our longing for peace and happiness. As the poet John O'Donohue said, 'There is a place in you where you have never been wounded.'* He was referring to our essential self, pure being. Being is our refuge. It is the place of peace. It is the experience that gives us the peace and quiet joy for which we long.

No experience, however refined or spiritual, can ever truly satisfy our thirst for peace and happiness. It is only the knowledge of our essential self that has this thirst-quenching power.

No object, activity, circumstance or relationship can give us what we truly long for, which is only our being. No teacher or teaching can give us the peace and happiness that are the nature of our self. Nor need they, because we already *are* that. To expect someone or something other than our self to provide us with the peace and happiness for which we long is to set ourselves up for disappointment and failure.

Nothing and no one can make us happy. Peace and happiness are the nature of being, and we are that.

In fact, everyone tastes the peace and quiet joy that is our nature numerous times throughout the day. For instance,

* Krista Tippet, host, *On Being*, podcast, 'The Inner Landscape of Beauty' (February 28, 2008).

every time a thought or feeling comes to an end, a desire is fulfilled, we are astonished or amazed, or we are touched by love, we briefly taste our true nature of simply being and experience its innate peace and quiet joy. Our being is tasting itself, so to speak.

Thus, the experiences of peace, happiness and love are interventions of our being in the flow of experience, like the clouds briefly parting and allowing the blue sky to shine through. The experiences of peace, happiness and love are the shining of being in the midst of experience.

*   *   *

Just as the physical space in a room is inherently devoid of any objects, so our being is inherently empty of the content of experience.

As it is inherently empty of objective content, being does not share the agitation that characterises our thoughts. Like empty space, it cannot be disturbed and thus its nature is peace.

As it is inherently empty, being is devoid of the sorrow that characterises our feelings, and thus its nature is happiness or quiet joy.

As it is inherently empty, being is devoid of the divisions and limitations that characterise experience. It is infinite. It is the one being from which everyone and everything derives its apparently independent existence.

At the level of people and things, there is otherness and separation. For being, there is just its own infinite, indivisible self. This utter absence of division or separation is the experience of love. As the Sufi mystic Awhad al-din Balyani said, 'Other than Him is Him without any otherness'.*

Being does not need to be made peaceful, happy or loving through practice, effort or discipline; it may simply be recognised as such.

*   *   *

Let us return to our analogy of the water.

If we were to take a cup of tea and remove the tea, the milk, the honey and so on, what would remain? Just water. If we remove from ourself any element of experience that is not essential to us, what remains? Simply being.

Only our essential self, the water of the self, remains. It is tasteless, colourless, transparent, without name or form, and yet it satisfies our thirst for peace and happiness.

So-called enlightenment or awakening is not an extraordinary experience that happens to us. It is simply the recognition of the nature of being. It is our self's clear knowing of itself before it is 'coloured' or 'endarkened' by experience. It is simply the clear shining of being, the pure knowledge 'I am'.

---

* Ibn 'Arabi/Balyani, *Know Yourself: An Explanation of the Oneness of Being*, trans. by Cecilia Twinch (Beshara Publications, 2011).

When water is mixed with tea, it appears darker and denser, although nothing actually happens to the water itself. It remains as it essentially is. Likewise, when our being is mixed with the content of experience, it seems to become darker and denser. Its original transparency seems lost. Being seems to become endarkened by experience. We become sorrowful, agitated, lonely and so on. But being always remains as it essentially is: pure, transparent, silent and still. We remain as we essentially are.

Being is never endarkened by experience and, therefore, does not need to be enlightened by practice.

Being may be concealed and revealed, forgotten and remembered, or ignored and recognised, but its nature never changes.

Meditation or prayer is simply the means by which we recognise the transparency of our essential self. Our self recognises itself. In meditation or prayer, nothing is added to us. Indeed, nothing is removed from us. We simply stand as we eternally are: transparent, empty, luminous.

Our essential being is always shining with the same brightness; it only seems to be dimmed or endarkened by experience. When clouds dissipate, the sun seems to shine more brightly. But in fact, the sun always shines with the same intensity. Likewise, as we travel back through the layers of experience, discarding everything that is not essential to us, our being seems to shine more brightly. But in fact, our being always shines with the same intensity and luminosity.

It only seems to be obscured by experience. This shining of being is the essence of meditation or prayer.

If our attention is absorbed in thinking, it is not necessary to turn away from the experience. We do not need to try to stop thinking. We simply notice, 'I am thinking', and emphasise the 'I am' rather than the thinking.

If our attention is lost in a feeling, such as sadness or loneliness, it is not necessary to stop feeling. We simply notice, 'I am feeling sad' or 'I am lonely', and emphasis the 'I am' rather than the feeling.

Take any experience and see that the 'I am' is always shining there. If I am depressed, the 'I am' is shining there. If I am ecstatic, the 'I am' is shining there. If I am lonely, the 'I am' is shining there. Instead of trying to avoid or get rid of the depression or loneliness, we go deeply into it and find the 'I am' shining there. We taste the water in the wine.

In everyday life, experience obscures being. In meditation or prayer, being outshines experience.

CHAPTER 3

FALLING ASLEEP WHILST REMAINING AWAKE

All that God asks of us, most pressingly, is that
we go out of ourself and let God be God in us.
MEISTER ECKHART

When everything that can be removed from us is removed, what we essentially are shines by itself.

No thought, feeling or perception is essential to us. These all appear, exist briefly, and then vanish. What remains when each of these has vanished? Simply being, being aware or awareness itself. Only that qualifies as our essential, irreducible self.

Let us explore this in our own experience. The revelation of our true nature could be likened to falling asleep at night whilst remaining awake.

When we fall asleep at night, initially perceptions leave us. That is, sights, sounds, tastes, textures and smells disappear. As a result, our experience of the world disappears.

Then sensations leave us, and the experience of the body disappears. This leaves us in the dream state, aware only of thoughts and images.

Eventually thoughts and images disappear, leaving us all alone as pure being. Instead of the awareness of experience, all that remains is the awareness of being. We are not aware of ourself as a man, a woman or even a person; we are just aware of being. That is, being is aware of itself. We refer to this as 'deep sleep'. As such, deep sleep is not the absence of awareness; it is the awareness of absence. It is the shining of being, all by itself.

*   *   *

Even to say that deep sleep is the awareness of absence is a concession to the object-knowing mind. The object-knowing mind is not present in deep sleep, so there are no objects of experience there, or even any memory of them. Since it is devoid of any objects, or even any memory of them, deep sleep cannot be said to be an absence. It is only an absence of objects from the point of view of the object-knowing mind. But in being's experience of itself, deep sleep is simply the shining of its own presence, all alone.

To illustrate this, let us consider an example. Imagine that a friend has just given you a lift home from the airport after you have been away for two weeks. You both walk into the house, and the first thing you notice is that your favourite painting is missing. You exclaim, 'It's missing!'

'What's missing?' your friend replies.

You point to the wall. Your friend looks at the wall, bewildered. She just sees the wall as it is. Nothing is missing.

You see the absence of a painting only in reference to your memory of it. Your friend has no memory of the paining and, therefore, does not see its absence. She just sees the presence of the wall.

The same is true of deep sleep. The object-knowing mind refers to deep sleep as an absence only in reference to its memory of objects. Being experiences deep sleep as it is in itself, without any reference to memory. All that is there is its own presence.

In other words, we normally think that deep sleep is the absence of awareness. To counter this belief, we first suggest that it is not the absence of awareness but the awareness of absence. When the mind has fully considered this possibility, we then take the next step. It is not even the awareness of absence. It is simply the awareness of being, the shining of being, all alone.

*   *   *

Meditation or prayer is the means by which we return to our true nature. In meditation or prayer, we sink deeper and deeper into being, much like falling asleep whilst remaining awake.

When we fall asleep, we don't get rid of thoughts, sensations and perceptions; we just let them go. Likewise, in meditation or prayer, we don't eliminate any element of experience; we just let it go.

Just as we do not make an effort to fall asleep but rather relax all previous efforts, so in meditation or prayer, we relax all previous efforts to do, to acquire, to become, to know.

Everything that is not essential to us leaves us, without any effort on our part.

Having said that, if we find ourself lost in the drama of experience, we should make the gentle effort to extricate ourself from it and come back to simply being. In time, the content of experience will begin to lose its power over us, and we will find ourself effortlessly remaining in being, as being.

Simply being is our natural condition prior to experience. It is our refuge, our home.

*   *   *

One way to initiate this effortless meditation is to ask oneself, 'What remains of my self when everything that can be removed from me is removed from me?' What am I in the absence of experience, that is, in the absence of thoughts, feelings, sensations and perceptions? Or, what element of my experience remains continually present throughout the three states of waking, dreaming and sleeping?

Only *that* qualifies as your essential self.

The essence of anything is the aspect of that thing that cannot be removed from it. For instance, water cannot be removed from a wave and is, as such, its essence, relatively speaking. Likewise, the essence of our self is the aspect of our self that cannot be removed from us.

Imagine removing from your self everything that can be removed, namely, thoughts, feelings, sensations and perceptions.

What remains? Pure being. In meditation or prayer, we simply abide as that.

In fact, it is not necessary to actually remove the content of experience. We simply trace our way back through the layers of experience to our essential self.

What we essentially are is not created or acquired as a result of this process. Being was previously concealed; now it is revealed. It was previously forgotten; now it is remembered.

By 'remembered', I do not mean to imply a memory of something from the past. It is, rather, the 'memory' of something that lies deep within us now, and at all times, but is usually overlooked or forgotten. The practice that is referred to as 'self-remembering' is simply to abide in being, as being.

Even to say 'abide as that' is a compassionate concession to the one who seems to be *other* than that. Being does not need to practise abiding as itself. It is already itself. It cannot be anything else.

Simply know yourself as that, and be that knowingly.

*   *   *

When you fall asleep, the mind, the body and the world leave you, and you remain as you essentially are: pure being. In fact, when you fall asleep at night, you don't really fall asleep. Perceptions, sensations, thoughts and images leave you, and you remain as you are: wide awake, aware of nothing other than being. There is just the awareness of being, and you are that without being 'you' and without that being 'that'.

In other words, the transition from the waking state to the dream state, and from the dream state to deep sleep, seems to be a transition that we, as a person, pass through. However, from the point of view of being, this apparent transition is simply the process by which everything that is not essential to it – perceptions, sensations, thoughts and images – is removed from it, leaving it all alone as it essentially is.

In deep sleep, we never think, 'This is not enough', or 'I want to be enlightened'. We never feel upset or hurt. It is for this reason that we all look forward to sleep at night. In deep sleep, we simply abide in being, as being. Being abides in itself, as itself.

In simply being, the turmoil that characterises our thoughts is not present, and thus there is no agitation. The sorrow that characterises our feelings is not present, and thus there is no suffering. The absence of agitation is the experience we know as peace; the absence of suffering is the experience we know as happiness.

Peace and happiness are not derived from the content of experience. They are the nature of our being. They are prior to, and independent of, whatever is taking place in our experience. They are the imperturbable peace and causeless joy that 'passeth all understanding'.*

* Philippians 4:7

*　　*　　*

We could also liken this effortless meditation to undressing at night. When we get undressed at night, we take off everything that is not essential to us. We take off all our clothes, leaving our naked body revealed. We do not suddenly become our naked body; we are always our naked body, relatively speaking, although we may not notice it during the day because it is covered in clothes.

In effortless meditation or prayer, we 'undress' our self. We take off the layers of experience that are not essential to us, leaving our naked being revealed. We do not become naked being as a result of this process; we are always that, although we may not notice it due to the exclusive focus of our attention on the content of experience. When our being is no longer clothed in experience, our essential self is simply revealed.

Likewise, when we wake up in the morning, we put on our clothes, thereby obscuring our naked body. But nothing actually happens to our body. It remains as it is. Similarly, in everyday life, when we wake up, our naked being is clothed in experience. But its nature never changes. It remains as it essentially is: ever-present, shining quietly behind and in the midst of all experience.

*　　*　　*

On the Pathless Path, meditation or prayer is not something we do; it is what we are. It is simply to abide as that which remains when all perceptions, sensations, thoughts and images have been removed from us.

As Meister Eckhart said, 'When I am able to establish myself in nothing and nothing in myself, uprooting and casting out what is in me, then I can pass into the naked being of God, which is the naked being of the Spirit.'*

To 'establish myself in nothing' is to abide in naked being, as naked being. To 'uproot and cast out everything that is in me' is to remove, so to speak, all the garments of experience. It is to gently let go of thoughts, feelings, perceptions and so on.

As our being sheds the qualities that it borrows from the content of experience, it loses its apparent limitations. The finite being that we seem to be stands revealed as pure being, shining all by itself, transparent, silent, still. Our being is revealed as infinite being, God's being, the only being there is.

The consummate knowledge, and the ultimate prayer, is simply to stand as naked being, divested of the qualities we derive from the content of experience. It is to abide as we are, naked, empty and free.

In meditation or prayer, we shed everything that is superfluous to us. We pass through the eye of the needle. We become as nothing.

The emptiness that we are is the fullness that God is.

* * *

* Meister Eckhart, *Complete Mystical Works, op. cit*

Just as meditation or prayer involves falling asleep whilst remaining awake, we could say that everyday life involves waking up whilst remaining asleep.

By 'remaining asleep' in this context, I mean remaining as pure being. By 'waking up', I mean the waking up of experience within us – that is, the arising of thoughts, sensations and perceptions. So, by 'waking up whilst remaining asleep', I mean remaining as being in the midst of all experience.

When we fall asleep, we don't really fall asleep. Thoughts, sensations and perceptions simply leave us. Likewise, when we wake up, we don't really wake up. Thoughts, sensations and perceptions are simply added to us.

When thoughts and images are added to us, we refer to it as 'the dream state'. When sensations and perceptions are further added to us, we refer to it as 'the waking state'. But we do not really pass from deep sleep to the dream state, or from the dream state to the waking state. The states pass through us; we don't pass through them. We remain as we eternally are.

Likewise, the transition from the waking state to the dream state, and from the dream state to deep sleep, seems to be a transition that we, as a person, pass through. In fact, this apparent transition is the process whereby we, as pure being, are divested of everything that is not essential to us, leaving us all alone.

We don't really wake up; experience wakes up in us. We don't fall asleep; experience is simply removed from us.

Being never enters into, or passes through, any states. It simply remains unchanged, as it eternally is.

Having said that, when experience wakes up in us, our being mixes with it so thoroughly that it loses touch with itself as it essentially is. Infinite being seems to acquire the limitations that characterise our experience and, as a result, seems to become a finite being. God's being seems to become a human being without ever actually ceasing to be itself.

If the art of meditation or prayer is to return to our essential being, then the art of life is to remain as being in the midst of all experience. In so doing, we remain in touch with the peace and quiet joy that are our true nature. At the same time, we feel our being as the same being that appears as everyone and everything. In other words, we love everyone and everything as appearances of the one infinite being, God's being, the divine.

*   *   *

Being is in the same relationship to experience as a screen is to a movie. The screen is present before the movie begins. However, when the movie begins, the screen is not changed or tarnished by it. It remains as it is: clear and transparent.

Likewise, our being is present prior to the arising of experience. However, when experience begins, our being is not changed, harmed or tarnished by it. It remains as it essentially is: silent, still, at peace. We participate fully in experience whilst remaining 'deeply asleep', that is, whilst remaining in the peace of our true nature.

We remain wide awake in deep sleep and deeply asleep whilst wide awake.

Simply being is like a current that runs continually throughout our lives, irrespective of our circumstances. To remain as that in the midst of experience is, in the Orthodox Christian tradition, referred to as 'praying without ceasing'. Brother Lawrence referred to it as 'the practice of the presence of God'.* It is to remain in touch with the 'I am' at all times and under all circumstances. We remain as we are: being only being, knowing only being, loving only being.

As Meister Eckhart said, 'Our whole life ought to be being. So far as our life is being, so far it is in God.'†

---

* *The Practice of the Presence of God: The Original 17th Century Letters and Conversations of Brother Lawrence* (XULON Press, 2007).
† Meister Eckhart, *Complete Mystical Works, op. cit.*

CHAPTER 4

I ETERNALLY AM

The face you had before you were born is your original face.
ZEN PROVERB

What is our most fundamental experience? Simply being. Is there any experience prior to simply being? If there were an experience prior to simply being, we would have to *be* there to know it. Therefore, being is our primary experience.

Do we need to do anything special in order to be, or is being freely given? Does being need to be manufactured or maintained by practice? Does being *practise* being?

Simply being is not a special state. It is not something we must practise. We do not need to make an effort to be. Being is what we naturally, effortlessly *are*; it is not what we *do*.

Being is our natural condition. It is what the Zen tradition refers to as 'our original face'. It is what we essentially are before layers of experience have been added to us.

Do we need to stop doing anything in particular in order to be? For instance, do we need to stop thinking, feeling or acting in order to simply be?

Is being ever aggrandised or diminished by experience?

Can the experience of simply being ever be disturbed, or does it shine quietly, unperturbed, behind and in the midst of all experience?

Does the experience of simply being ever undergo any change? Is the current experience of simply being different from the experience of simply being two minutes ago, two years ago or when we were two-year-old infants? Is simply being a different experience for the saint and for the sinner, or is it always the same experience?

Just as the screen remains present behind and throughout a movie without being changed by it, so being remains present behind and in the midst of all experience without being modified, tarnished or aged by it.

*　　*　　*

To explore this in your own experience, imagine you are a newborn infant. You have just been born but, of course, do not know you have just been born. Your eyes are still closed, and the room is quiet, so you have no experience of the world. A few mild sensations are present, but you do not experience them as sensations 'of a body'. You do not know that you are a body or that you have a body.

There are no thoughts or memories to refer to. You know nothing of time or space. You have no name. You do not know that you are a boy or a girl. You do not even have the experience of being a human being, but you do have the experience of being.

In fact, being is not an experience that you, as a person, have. It is you, being, that has the experience of being. You do not even know that you are 'you'. You have no sense of being a self or having a self. There is only being, and you are that without being 'you'.

For you, being, there is no time, no space, no person, no body, no world. There is just your self, all alone. There is just the luminosity of being, shining all by itself.

*   *   *

In the experience of simply being, there are no thoughts and, therefore, no agitation. This absence of agitation, which is the very nature of being, will later be conceptualised as 'peace'.

In the experience of simply being, there is no sorrow, lack or unhappiness. As such, simply being is inherently free of any dissatisfaction or suffering. Being is whole, perfect and complete. This fullness and sufficiency, which is the very nature of being, will later be conceptualised as 'happiness'.

In a collection of poems by William Blake, *Songs of Innocence*, he evokes this understanding in a poem, 'Infant Joy':

'I have no name;
I am but two days old.'
What shall I call thee?
'I happy am,
Joy is my name.'
Sweet joy befall thee!

This deceptively simple poem echoes the understanding that lies at the heart of all the great religious and spiritual traditions, namely, that joy is the very nature of being.

Thus, peace and happiness are the natural condition of our essential self, pure being. They belong to our original innocence. Agitation, sorrow and separation belong to experience.

If being were to give itself a name, it would call itself 'I', for 'I' is the name that that which knows itself gives to itself.

But for now, imagining yourself as a newborn baby, being has not yet given itself a name. It is nameless and formless and, as such, stands as the infinite whose nature is peace, joy and love.

* * *

Now fast-forward to your deathbed. You have a couple of minutes to live. Your eyes are closed, the room is dark and silent, and your body is comfortable. There are no sensations, so you do not experience being a body or having a body.

You have completely lost your memory. There are no thoughts. You have no experience of the world. You do not know that you were born, have lived a full life and are about to die. You do not even have the experience of being a human being, but you do have the experience of being. There is only the awareness of being, and you are that without being 'you'.

Lying on your deathbed, experience is dying in you. But you, pure being, have no experience of dying. You remain as you eternally are while all experience leaves you.

That which cannot be removed from us, the fact of simply being, remains as it eternally is. I eternally am.

Divested of the qualities that being derives from the content of experience, it stands naked, empty, free and at peace. Might Blake have added a supplementary verse?

> 'I have no name;
> I am one hundred years old.'
> What shall I call thee?
> 'I peaceful am,
> Peace is my name.'
> Eternal peace be with thee!

When you close your eyes for the last time, your breath slows down and eventually ceases. Your heart stops beating, and people will say that you have died. But you have not changed; you, being, remain unaffected.

Experience has died in you, but you have not died in experience. Being remains as it eternally is.

*   *   *

What is the difference between the experience of simply being two minutes after we were born, and the experience of simply being two minutes before we die?

In the intervening years, there were innumerable thoughts, memories, feelings, sensations and perceptions. We engaged in many activities and relationships. These changed countless times, but did the experience of being change? In other words, did your essential nature change? Is our being modified, hurt, tarnished or aged by the content of experience? Or is our being when we are on our deathbed in exactly the same pristine, innocent condition as it is just after we are born?

For the mind, decades have passed between these two samples of being: the sample of being a few moments after we are born, and the sample of being a few moments before we die. For being, no time has passed. They are the same moment, which is not a moment in time. It is eternity.

On our deathbed, we may suddenly realise, 'I never went anywhere; I never did anything; no time has passed; I am now as I always was and always will be, in eternity.' At that moment, we speak on behalf of being. For being, no time has passed between these two moments. They are the same moment, this moment, the eternal now.

*   *   *

This moment is not a moment in time. The experience we refer to as 'time' is the shining of being, refracted through thought. For the mind, there is a journey through time: our life progresses from the moment we were born to the moment we die. This is the horizontal line of time along which our life unfolds. However, being does not exist in that dimension; being is a vertical dimension that intersects the horizontal line of time. The experience we refer to as 'now' is the intersection between these two realms. For the mind, 'now' is a moment in time. For being, the same 'now' is eternity.

Likewise, the experience we refer to as 'space' is the shining of being, refracted through perception. For the mind, there is a journey through space. For being, there is only the infinite. The experience that we refer to as 'here' is the intersection of these two realms. For the mind, 'here' is a place in space. However, for being, the same 'here' is not a place in space. It is its own placeless, dimensionless presence. It is the placeless place where I, being, eternally am.

The American poet E. E. Cummings expressed this in his poem 'Love Is A Place':

> love is a place
> & through this place of
> love move
> (with brightness of peace)
> all places
>
> yes is a world
> & in this world of
> yes live
> (skilfully curled)
> all worlds*

The 'here and now' is a portal through which the mind passes out of space and time into the infinite and eternal.

The infinite and the eternal are not extraordinary mystical realms to which a few remarkable people have access. They are the very nature of the being that each of us now is.

* 'Love Is A Place', from *Complete Poems 1904–1962* (Liveright, 2016).

We are not born into time and space; time and space are born in us.

We have no experience of being born; experience is born in us.

When experience is born in us, the mind goes on an apparent journey through time and space. For the mind, there is birth, aging, sickness and death. Being knows nothing of such things. For being, there is simply the shining of its own ever-presence.

*   *   *

The experience of simply being is the changeless background of our continually changing experience. It is the invisible thread on which the pearls of experience are strung. Our whole life is a movement from being to being, which is no movement at all. We are not born, we do not grow old, and we do not die.

Can being ever disappear?

Anything that disappears must disappear into the medium within which it has arisen. A wave subsides into the ocean; a movie vanishes into the screen.

What would being disappear into? Non-being?

In order for being to disappear into non-being, non-being would have to *be*. In order for being to emerge from non-being, non-being would have to *be*. Being does not arise from anything or disappear into anything. It eternally is. From its own point of view, I eternally am.

*　　*　　*

To illustrate this, consider the space of a room. The space of a room does not come into existence when the room is built, and it does not go out of existence when the room is demolished. When the room is built, the space seems to acquire the size and shape of the four walls but, in fact, always remains the same unlimited, universal space. When the room is demolished, nothing happens to the space. It is not suddenly liberated from the four walls. It was never limited by them in the first place. The space remains as it always is.

Likewise, being does not begin or come into existence when our human experience begins. Being does not die or go out of existence when experience comes to an end. Being does not need to be liberated from the content of experience, because it was never bound by it in the first place. Being stands eternally free.

Being is never conditioned or qualified by experience and, therefore, does not need to be liberated. It is never 'endarkened' by experience and, therefore, does not need to be enlightened. It may be concealed and revealed, overlooked and recognised, forgotten and remembered, but always remains shining as it is.

This forgetting or overlooking of our true nature of simply being is expressed by William Wordsworth in this passage from his poem, 'Ode: Intimations of Immortality'. Wordsworth describes how the experience of simply being fades 'into the light of common day'. That is, the experience of simply being is veiled by the perceptions and activities of the waking state. In his words,

> Our birth is but a sleep and a forgetting:
> The Soul that rises with us, our life's Star,
> Hath had elsewhere its setting,
> And cometh from afar:
> Not in entire forgetfulness,
> And not in utter nakedness,
> But trailing clouds of glory do we come
> From God, who is our home:
> Heaven lies about us in our infancy!
> Shades of the prison-house begin to close
> Upon the growing Boy,
> But He beholds the light, and whence it flows,
> He sees it in his joy;
> The Youth, who daily farther from the east
> Must travel, still is Nature's Priest,
> And by the vision splendid
> Is on his way attended;
> At length the Man perceives it die away,
> And fade into the light of common day.*

The waking state is, as such, a state of amnesia, a sleep, a forgetting, a dream. To 'remember' our self, the fact of simply being, is to wake up from this dream of forgetfulness. It is to return to infinite being, God's being, 'who is our home'.

---

* 'Ode: Intimations of Immortality from Recollections of Early Childhood', from *Poems, in Two Volumes*, 1807.

*   *   *

Now, come to your present experience. You are currently aware of thoughts, feelings, sensations and perceptions. As a result, the experience of being may have receded into the background and, with it, its innate peace. However, your being is not changed by the content of your current experience.

At every moment of experience, being shines. This simple understanding is concealed in common parlance, 'I am cooking breakfast', 'I am lonely', 'I am going to work' and so on. It is always the same 'I am' qualified by an activity, feeling, idea or relationship. Being remains as it is, shining brightly in the midst of all experience: luminous, free, untarnished, innocent, inherently peaceful and unconditionally fulfilled.

Can any experience ever truly obscure the shining of being? Is the screen veiled by the movie, or does it shine *as* the movie? It depends on how we look at it. Is being concealed by our experience, or does it shine *in* and *as* our experience? It depends on how we look at it. We are free to allow our activities and feelings to veil our being, in which case, they will seem to do so. Or, we are free to remain in touch with being, as being, in which case its innate peace and quiet joy will remain present throughout the day.

At any moment of experience, we can return to our being and remain as that. We stand there together in eternity, as one and in peace.

CHAPTER 5

OUR PORTAL TO REALITY

Whosoever knows their self, knows their Lord.
SUFI SAYING

Everything we know about the universe is filtered through the finite mind – that is, the faculties of thinking and perceiving. These faculties are limited and, therefore, everything we know about the universe appears in accordance with their limitations. Our perceiving faculties of seeing, hearing, touching, tasting and smelling confer their limitations onto the reality of the world, making it appear in the form of sights, sounds, tastes, textures and smells. As William Blake said,

> This life's dim windows of the soul
> Distort the heavens from pole to pole
> And lead you to believe a lie
> When you see with, not through the eye.*

'This life's dim windows of the soul' are our perceiving faculties – our eyes, ears and so on – and 'the heavens' is Blake's traditional name for reality. We cannot know reality through our perceiving faculties, just as one cannot see white snow through orange-tinted glasses.

* *The Book of Thel*, 1789.

When it is said in the great religious and spiritual traditions that the world is an illusion, it does not mean that the world is not real. It simply means that the *reality* of the world is not what it *appears* to be. It appears to be a multiplicity and diversity of finite objects made of matter. Why does the world appear like this? Because we see it through the lens of sense perception.

What is the reality of the world? Infinite being. The world derives its *reality* from infinite being and its *appearance* from the finite mind. The world is, as such, the interface between infinite being and the finite mind. In other words, the infinite appears as the finite when filtered through the faculties of perception.

It is for this reason that William Wordsworth suggested we 'half create and half perceive' the world.* We 'half create' the world in the sense that our perceiving faculties confer their own limitations onto the reality of the world, thereby creating its appearance. We 'half perceive' the world in the sense that we are *experiencing* what it truly is, albeit filtered through the medium of sense perception. In this sense, the world is both illusory and real. Just as a mirage in the desert is illusory as a pool of water but real, relatively speaking, as a play of light, so the world is illusory as a multiplicity and diversity of objects made of matter but real as infinite being. As the Zen master

* *Lines Composed a Few Miles above Tintern Abbey, On Revisiting the Banks of the Wye during a Tour, July 13, 1798* (1798)

Huang Po said, people 'neglect the reality of the "illusory" world'.*

If we look at snow through orange-tinted glasses, we see orange snow. The orange snow derives its reality, relatively speaking, from the white snow. It borrows its appearance from the orange glasses through which it is perceived. Likewise, the world derives its reality from infinite being. It borrows its appearance from the finite mind through which it is perceived.

The finite mind confers name and form on reality. Thought gives reality its names; perception gives it its forms. Divested of the names and forms that thought and perception confer on reality, only infinite being remains.

*   *   *

If everything known through the finite mind shares its limitations, could we ever know the nature of reality as it essentially is?

Just as one cannot know white snow through orange-tinted glasses, we cannot know the nature of reality when we look at it through the lens of perception. If we explore the nature of reality through the finite mind, the best we can say is 'I don't know whether reality is limited. The infinite may exist, but I have no knowledge of it'. It was

* *The Zen Teaching of Huang Po: On the Transmission of Mind,* translated by John Blofeld (Grove Press, 1958).

in this context that Socrates said, 'I know that I know nothing'.*

Is it possible, then, to know the nature of reality? It would only be possible through an experience that is not mediated by the finite mind and, therefore, does not share its limitations. In other words, we can only know reality through an experience that is not filtered through thought or perception. Is there such an experience?

The only experience that is not mediated through the filters of thought and perception is the experience of being, that is, the knowledge 'I am'. The knowledge 'I am' seems to be an experience *in* the finite mind and seems, as such, to take place in time and space. But when we go deeply into the experience 'I am', we pass, as it were, through a portal in the mind. We pass out of time into eternity; we pass out of space into the infinite.

In this way, the awareness of being, or the knowledge 'I am', is the only knowledge in which we have direct, unmediated access to reality. It's like a beacon in the mind that indicates the reality beyond it. As such, the knowledge 'I am' is our portal to reality, our 'dream-ladder to divinity'.†

*   *   *

To illustrate this, consider a watercolour painting by the English painter William Turner. It is a painting of a land-

---

* Thought to be a paraphrase of a statement in Plato's 'Apology'.
† David Whyte, *Everything is Waiting for You*, (Many Rivers Press, 2003).

scape at night, illuminated by the full moon. The landscape consists of fields, trees, animals and so on. In the top left-hand corner of the painting, the full moon is shining. The light of the moon suffuses the entire painting and illuminates the landscape.

As we explore the painting, our attention is first drawn to the trees, animals and other objects in the landscape. In time, we notice the full moon. At first glance, the moon seems to be an object *in* the landscape. However, upon closer examination, we realise that the moon is the *only* part of the paper that hasn't been painted. It is just the white paper and, as such, is not *in* the painting at all. In other words, what appears as the full moon is not really a moon. It's the white paper, the background of the entire painting.

The knowledge 'I am' is like the moon in Turner's painting. At first, the knowledge 'I am' seems to be an object of experience *in* the mind. It seems to be a temporary experience that comes and goes along with all other experience. However, as we go deeply into the knowledge 'I am', we discover that it is not an experience *in* the mind, just as the moon is not an object *in* the painting.

Just as the moon is not an object in the landscape but a gap through which the white paper is visible, so the knowledge 'I am' is a gap in the mind through which infinite being shines. The knowledge 'I am' is the shining of being, uncoloured by the mind. It is the only *part* of experience that remains, as it were, 'unpainted' by experience.

In other words, when we go into the moon, we go out of the moon. We discover the white paper that is the background of the entire painting. Likewise, when we go deeply into ourself, we go out of ourself.

When we go deeply into the knowledge 'I am', which seems to reside in the finite mind, we are divested of the limitations that we borrow from the content of experience and stand revealed as infinite being. The deeper we delve into our being, the more the sense of a separate self dissolves.

*　　*　　*

The infinite leaves a trace of itself in each of our finite minds as the knowledge 'I am'. In religious language, we could say that God shines in each of our minds as the knowledge 'I am'.

'I am' is God's signature in each of our minds.

As such, the knowledge 'I am' shines as a beacon of freedom amidst the sea of experience. It gives the finite mind a hint as to where to look in order to know the nature of reality. The knowledge 'I am' is, as such, a portal through which the finite mind must pass if it wants to know reality.

The knowledge 'I am' stands at the threshold between the finite and the infinite, just as a prison door stands at the threshold between captivity and freedom. We can pass through a prison door in two directions. As we pass through the door from the prison into the outside world, we lose the limitations that were imposed on us and regain our inherent freedom. When we pass through the same door in the opposite direction, we temporarily acquire the limitations of the prison and, as a result, lose our freedom.

When a man passes through the prison door to the outside world, he sheds the restrictions that were imposed on him and regains his freedom. Likewise, as the finite mind passes through the portal 'I am', it is divested of the qualities that it borrows from experience and stands revealed as the infinite.

When a man passes through the prison door to the outside world, he ceases to be an inmate and becomes a free man. Likewise, as the finite mind passes through the portal 'I am', it loses its limitations – 'I am *tired*', 'I am *lonely*', 'I am *sad*' and so forth – and the 'I am' shines naked, alone and free.

In fact, the man doesn't become free on leaving prison; he was always free, but the prison regime was temporarily imposed on him. Likewise, our being doesn't become free when it loses the limitations that experience imposes on it. It is simply revealed as such.

As the finite mind passes through this portal 'I am', it sheds its faculties of thinking and perceiving. As a result, time and space disappear. We slip out of time and enter eternity. We fall through a crack in the world and stand as the infinite.

The knowledge 'I am' is the last outpost of the finite mind. It is the doorway to the infinite.

As long as the 'I am' remains unqualified, it refers to infinite being and is, as such, an expression of the highest truth.

*   *   *

What happens when the man passes through the same door in the opposite direction, from the outside world into the prison? He loses his inherent freedom, and the prison regime is imposed on him. Likewise, as soon as infinite being passes through the doorway 'I am', it becomes qualified by experience. 'I am' becomes 'I am *tired*', 'I am *lonely*', 'I am *sad*'and so forth. In doing so, it seems to acquire limitations. The pure 'I am' becomes 'I am this' or 'I am that'. In this case, the knowledge 'I am' is the first seed of limitation, which later grows into our experience of sorrow and separation. In this case, the knowledge 'I am' is the seed of ignorance.*

As infinite being passes through the portal 'I am', it is mixed with experience. It leaves eternity and is born in time and space. It is in this context that Wordsworth said, 'Our birth is but a sleep and a forgetting'.† Infinite being seems to become a finite being or separate self.

The knowledge 'I am' is the portal between the infinite and the finite. It stands at the threshold between the highest knowledge and the deepest ignorance. It is in this context

---

* *Ignorance*, in this context, simply refers to the ignoring or overlooking of our essential being.
† 'Ode: Intimations of Immortality from Recollections of Early Childhood', from *Poems, in Two Volumes,* 1807.

that J. Krishnamurti referred to 'the first and last freedom'.*
For the person, 'I am' is the knowledge through which we
gain our inherent freedom. It is, as such, our 'first freedom'.
However, for being, it is the same knowledge 'I am', which,
when qualified by experience, leads to the loss of its inherent freedom. It is, as such, our 'last freedom'.

In other words, the knowledge 'I am' stands on the threshold between true knowledge and ignorance. When we cross
that threshold in one direction, our divinity is restored and,
with it, our immortality. When we cross the same threshold
in the opposite direction, we acquire the burden of experience and suffer accordingly. It is for this reason that Ramana
Maharshi referred to 'I am' as the highest knowledge and
Sri Nisargadatta Maharaj referred to the same knowledge
as the source of all ignorance.

In religious language, the knowledge 'I am' is the portal
through which a human being is divested of all temporary,
finite qualities and stands revealed as infinite being, God's
being, the only being there is. It is the same portal through
which infinite being passes in the opposite direction and is
born as a human being.

'I am' stands at the threshold between time and eternity.

*   *   *

Even to say that the finite mind must pass through the
portal 'I am' is a compassionate concession. In reality,

* J. Krishnamurti, *The First and Last Freedom*, (HarperSanFrancisco, 1975).

there is no finite mind that needs to pass through any portal. Just as Turner's moon does not need to *become* the white paper but is simply recognised as such, so the finite mind does not need to become infinite. Its essential nature is simply recognised as such. The space in a room *is* the vast space of the universe; it does not need to become it.

There is no becoming for being.

We cannot become what we essentially are; we cannot be what we are not.

Being eternally is as it is. I am always only I. As it is said in the Old Testament, 'I am that I am.'* In other words, God is identical to itself alone.

Our being is already infinite being; we do not need to become it. According to the Sufi saying, 'Whosoever knows their self, knows their Lord.' In other words, whosoever knows their self *as it truly is* knows that their being is infinite being, God's being, the only being there is.

Reflecting on this saying, Balyani observed that it does not say, whosoever '*annihilates* their self, knows their Lord'.† To suggest that a finite being or separate self needs to be annihilated requires first crediting it with an existence of its own. To do so is to set up a finite being alongside infinite being, and that is blasphemy.

* Exodus 3:14
† Ibn 'Arabi/Balyani, *op. cit.*

To illustrate this, imagine a sheet of white paper that represents infinite being. If we draw a line across the paper, we divide it into two, creating two finite spaces. Similarly, if we imagine a finite being existing alongside God, it would be as if a line had been drawn through infinite being, dividing it into two finite parts. Just as both spaces on the paper would be finite, both beings would be finite. And if God's being were finite, then God would not be God.

Ultimately, there is no finite being or separate self that emerges from God, exists in God, is separate from God or unites with God. There is just God's infinite being.

For this reason, this approach could be said to be a way of recognition or understanding. It is, as such, the Pathless Path. There is no path from our self to our self, just as there is no path from the moon to the white paper.

There is no pathway from the 'I am' that I am to the 'I am' that God is, for they are the same 'I am'.

The very being that each of us now is – that shines in us as the simple experience of 'being myself' or the knowledge 'I am' – is already the one infinite being. All that is required is to see that, and to be that knowingly.

CHAPTER 6

THE OUTSHINING OF EXISTENCE

The visible world is merely an
impermanent disguise worn by the eternal.
RABINDRANATH TAGORE

W e have recognised being as the common ground of our interior experience, but what about our exterior experience? If being is the essence of our self, what is the essence of the world?

Let us return to Turner's watercolour. We could say that the landscape in the painting exists, yet owes its reality, relatively speaking, to the white paper. The white paper underlies and pervades the entire landscape and is, as such, its substance or reality.

The objects in the landscape, such as the trees and animals, are transparent washes that colour the white paper, giving it a temporary name and form. But the reality of the landscape is the paper. Likewise, the common background of all objects and selves is being. As such, existence stands in the same relationship to being as does the painting to the white paper.

In other words, the white paper could be said to lend itself to the fields, trees and animals in the painting without ever actually becoming them. Likewise, being lends itself to all existent things without ever ceasing to be itself.

If we thinned the colours of any object in Turner's land-scape, be it a tree, a river or a person, we would discover the same white paper underneath. Imagine 'thinning the colours' of our sense perceptions. Imagine diluting the sights, sounds, tastes, textures and smells from our current experience of the world. What remains of the world? What 'stands behind' every sense perception?

Simply being.

* * *

The full moon is the only part of the painting that has not been covered by paint and is, as such, the place where the white paper shines at its brightest. However, if we look closely at the landscape, we see that the layers of transparent colour never completely obscure the paper. Although the white paper shines most brightly as the moon, it also shines *through* the entire landscape.

Likewise, the knowledge 'I am' is the only aspect of our experience that is not 'coloured' by thought and perception and is, as such, the experience in which being shines most brightly. However, if we go deeply into our experience of the world, we understand that being not only underlies but also shines through all existence.

The white paper shines in its purest form as the moon, but it also shines through and as the entire landscape. In the same way, God's infinite being shines in its brightest form as the knowledge 'I am', but also shines *through* and as the world.

Just as the paper is the common background of the entire painting and, therefore, does not share the qualities of any particular object in the painting, so being is the background of all things and, therefore, does not share the limited qualities of any particular thing. Being is, as such, infinite.

Just as the white paper has no form and, therefore, cannot be given a name with reference to any of the objects in the painting, so pure being has no form and, therefore, cannot legitimately be named. We could say that existence clothes being in names and forms.

Having no name or form, this background reality has no finite qualities. Finite qualities only pertain to existent things. This nameless, formless reality – from which everyone and everything emerge, in which they exist and into which they vanish – is infinite. It is infinite being, God's being, in which all seemingly separate people and things live and move and have their existence.*

*   *   *

Through what mechanism does existence emerge from being? Perception.

However, perception is not imposed on being from the outside. It is being itself that assumes the activity of perceiving. In doing so, being draws existence out of itself. It is through perception that it gives birth to its infinite potential in form. In other words, being assumes the activity of perceiving

---

* Acts 17:28

and, in doing so, gives birth to itself in form. Being gives birth to itself as the world through the act of perception.

Perception stands at the interface between the infinite and the finite. Every moment of perception is the lovemaking through which the infinite conceives the finite within itself.

It is perception that washes a thin layer of colour over infinite being, giving it the temporary name and form that we call 'the world'. As such, our sense perceptions colour, but never completely obscure, their reality.

However, it is not perception itself that veils reality. It is the *belief* that the objects are real in their own right that seems to veil reality. It is the belief that the landscape in the painting is a real landscape that seems to hide the white paper. As soon as that belief comes to an end, the landscape that once seemed to veil the white paper now shines with it. Likewise, as soon as the belief that the world is real in its own right comes to an end, it loses its concealing power and shines with being.

Everything shines with its reality for one who has eyes to see. When we look deeply into the world, all we find is the white paper, infinite being.

Perception colours infinite being, refracting it into an apparent multiplicity and diversity of objects and selves. However, in doing so, infinite being never becomes anything other than itself, just as the white paper never becomes the landscape.

We could say that the world is infinite being, clothed in name and form. This is what Blake meant when he said, 'Every bird that cuts the airy way is an immense world of delight, enclosed by the senses five.'* It is our perceiving faculties that enclose the 'immense world of delight' – infinite being – making it appear finite. God's infinite being, clothed in the names and forms that thinking and perceiving confer upon it, appears as a bird, a tree, a mountain or, indeed, the world. The world is the shining of being.

As such, being does not know the world as an object or an 'other'. It is utterly, intimately one with it. In fact, we cannot even say that it is utterly, intimately one with it because there is no 'it' for being to be intimate with. There is only the One, only infinite being. In other words, for being, the world is not really a world. It knows the world by being the world. This absence of otherness is love. In this sense, the world is an outpouring of love.

*   *   *

What is the difference between the full moon and the white paper? What is the difference between the being that is our essential nature and the being that is the ultimate reality of the universe? There is none. All the distinctions and divisions pertain to the content of experience – the names and forms – not to the white paper of infinite being.

* Blake, *op. cit.*

71

In giving our attention to the moon, we are giving our attention to the white paper. In giving our attention to the being that lies in the depths of our self, we are giving our attention to the being that is the substance and reality of the world.

There is one infinite, indivisible reality that, ultimately, cannot be named but could provisionally be referred to as being, God, Spirit, consciousness or love. It is the infinite being from which everything derives its apparently independent existence, without ever ceasing to be itself.

As Jesus said, 'I and My Father are one.'* 'I' is the moon, the experience of being that seems to reside inside us. 'My Father' is the white paper, God's infinite being, which seems to be outside us. They are one and the same. The 'I' that shines in the depths of our self *is* infinite being, the substance and reality of the world.

As Nagarjuna said, 'Nirvana and samsara are one.'† Just as the colourlessness of the white paper shines in Turner's painting as the full moon, so being's infinite nature shines in each of our minds as the knowledge 'I am'. Just as the white paper that is the essence of the moon is equally the essence of the landscape, so the being that is the essence of our self is the ultimate reality of the world.

* John 10:30
† *Mūlamadhyamakakārikā* (Fundamental Verses on the Middle Way), ch. 25.

As it is said in the Heart Sutra, 'Form is emptiness, and emptiness is form.' The moon is unpainted. It is colourless, empty of content. It is the white paper. However, the colourlessness of the white paper is the *reality* of the painting. Likewise, the empty, silent being that shines in the depths of each of our minds as the knowledge 'I am' is the reality of the world.

The emptiness of being is the fullness of the world.

*   *   *

When we go deeply into the knowledge 'I am', we discover the infinite being that is the background and reality of the entire world. This adds another layer to our understanding of the saying, 'Whosoever knows their self, knows their Lord.' We realise that whosoever knows the nature of their own being, knows the ultimate reality of the universe.

It is for this reason that a scientist who wants to know the nature of reality must eventually become a mystic. Whatever reality essentially *is* must be what we essentially *are*. The reality of the ocean, relatively speaking, is the same as the reality of the wave. To know the reality of the ocean, we need only explore a single wave. Likewise, to know the reality of the universe, we need only know the reality of our self. In fact, this is the *only* way to know the reality of the universe since our knowledge of our self is the only knowledge that is not mediated through the finite mind. Therefore, any scientist who wants to know the nature of the universe must go through their self – the portal 'I am' – not the world. As the artist Paul Gauguin reportedly said, 'I shut my eyes in order to see.'

Everything depends upon our knowledge of our self. We cannot know anything about the nature of the world until we know the nature of our self. It is through the moon that we have direct access to the white paper; it is through our self that we have direct access to reality. Any other experience is mediated through the finite mind and appears in accordance with that mind's limitations. Therefore, the knowledge 'I am' is the highest knowledge and the only knowledge that is absolutely true. All other knowledge is relative to the finite mind through which it is known.

Having recognised the nature of our self, we turn around and see the being that we essentially are shining in and as the world. The entire landscape shines with the white paper. Existence is the shining of being, the white radiance of eternity, and you are that without being 'you'.

*   *   *

Whatever we encounter inside of ourself is pervaded by the amness of being. Whatever seems to exist outside of ourself is pervaded by the isness of being. The amness that stands at the heart of all experience and the isness that stands at the heart of all existence is the same being.

Being conceals itself as experience on the inside; it veils itself as existence on the outside.

When we look inside, all we find is God's infinite being. When we look outside, all we find is God's infinite being. Just as the white paper extends beyond the apparent limitations of the full moon, our being extends beyond the apparent limitations of our individual bodies and minds. Being shines *as* the world.

In the Vedantic tradition, this recognition is referred to as 'sahaja samadhi': the revelation of the infinite in the finite. In the Tantric tradition, it is referred to as 'devouring our experience': the dissolution of experience in the transparency of being. In the Christian tradition, it is referred to as 'the transfiguration': the outshining of the world by the radiance of God's infinite being.

Previously, being was veiled *by* existence; now, being shines *as* existence.

As the radiance of being progressively outshines our experience, the distinction between meditation and everyday life fades. Meditation used to be a retreat from everyday life, and everyday life used to be a distraction from meditation. In meditation, our attention is absorbed in being at the expense of experience; in everyday life, our attention is lost in experience at the expense of being. However, in time, we cannot find a distinction between the two, just as we see the same white paper whether we are looking at the moon or the landscape.

In this transfiguration, our self is so emptied of itself that all that remains is God's infinite being, both within us and all around us.

We know our self as nothing and feel our self as everything. As Meister Eckhart said, 'As long as I am this or that...I am not all things.'*

When everything that can be removed from us is removed from us, our essential self shines as it is. This is the emptiness that Frances Nuttall offered to the divine when she said, 'Accept, Lord, this my emptiness, and so fill me with Thyself.'† It is what Abu-Saeed Abil-Kheir meant when he said, 'Until you become an unbeliever in your own self, you cannot become a believer in God.'‡

We allow the mind, the body and the world to become increasingly transparent to the luminosity that is the nature of our being. We allow all aspects of our experience to be progressively permeated with the light of being. We allow everything be suffused with the radiance of being, until it is gradually outshone by it.

In this transfiguration, the world becomes transparent to its reality. The world that once seemed to conceal its reality now shines with it. God's presence is no longer hidden behind the world but shines in and as it. As the Sufis say, 'All we see is the face of God.' All we hear is the song of being.

* My rendition from *The Complete Mystical Works of Meister Eckhart*, translated by Maurice O'C. Walshe.
† 'The Prayer of the Chalice' (1961).
‡ *Nobody Son of Nobody: Poems of Sheikh Abu-Saeed Abil-Kheir*, renditions by Vraje Abramian (Hohm Press, 2001).

CHAPTER 7

THE SONG OF BEING

*Nature is too thin a screen; the glory of the
omnipresent God bursts through everywhere.*
RALPH WALDO EMERSON

If our primary knowledge of ourself is the experience
of being, or the knowledge 'I am', then what is our
primary knowledge of any object?

Consider a tree, for instance. What is the first thing we
know about the tree?

Before we know anything about its size, shape or colour,
we know that it *is*.

Our primary knowledge of the tree is its isness or being.
Our primary knowledge of *any* object is simply its being.

This understanding is enshrined in our everyday language.
When we describe an object, we always start with 'it is'.
We say, '*it is* small', '*it is* large', '*it is* young', '*it is* old' and
so on. We always begin by affirming 'it *is*', and then we
add a temporary qualification. We start by affirming being.

Everything else we come to know about the object is added
to the 'it is': 'it is *small*', 'it is *large*', 'it is *young*', 'it is *old*'
and so on. It is always the same 'it is', qualified by a temporary state.

What is it that qualifies the 'it is'? Thought and perception. Thought gives the object its name; perception gives it its form. But what does the 'it is' refer to *before* it is qualified by thought and perception? What does the 'it is' refer to by itself?

The simple fact of being.

Before an object can have any temporary, finite qualities, it must first *be*. Before an object tells us anything about itself as an object, it first announces being. Every object shines with being.

*   *   *

It is for this reason that we enjoy walking in nature. When we walk in nature and see, for instance, a beautiful tree standing alone in a field, we are stopped in our tracks. What is it that is so compelling about the sight of the tree?

We are open and relaxed, free of the usual demands of everyday life, and suddenly we are struck by the tree's majestic stillness. The tree stands as an emblem of being. In that moment, we are thrown back into our true nature. The tree has lost its capacity to veil its reality and shines with being. In religious language, it shines with God's presence.

This is also one of the reasons we like to live with pets. While busy working in the house, we suddenly notice our cat lying on the windowsill, curled up in a pool of light. The cat is not practising being; it is simply resting in being. It is an image of being. When we encounter the cat lying quietly on the windowsill, our being resonates with its being. This interrupts our habitual stream of thoughts and feelings, and in that pause, our true nature of simply being shines.

It is for the same reason that we may place a beautiful bowl on a shelf. Why are we not satisfied with the pots and pans in our kitchen? It is because we associate them with function. We see the function we have assigned the object rather than the object as it is in itself. But the bowl on the shelf has no function. It has no reason to be there. The mind cannot do anything with it. Its presence interrupts our internal narrative, and in that pause, being shines.

I once sent two little beakers to a friend for his birthday. He mailed me a postcard in return, which read, 'I put your two little beakers on the mantelpiece in my living room and, as a result, had to tidy up my entire apartment.' Something about those two beakers had the power to cut through his usual mental patterns and had drawn him into simply being. Having tasted the peace of his true nature, he felt inspired to create a similar atmosphere of peace in his home.

We are surrounded everywhere by emblems of being. Everything shines with its reality.

*   *   *

What is the difference between our essential being on the inside and the being that is the essence of things – indeed, the essence of the universe – on the outside? What is the difference between the amness of our self and the isness of things?

This is like asking what the difference is between the space inside a room and the space outside it. There is just *one* space in the universe, seemingly divided by numerous separate buildings while, in fact, always remaining a single undivided space.

If the space inside a room were aware and could speak, it would say of itself, 'I am'. If it were to look out of the window at the vast space of the universe, it would say of that space, 'it is'. However, the amness of the space inside the room and the isness of the space outside the room are not two separate spaces. They are the same space. There is only one space, the vast space of the universe.

Likewise, our primary knowledge of ourself is 'I am'. When we look out of the window of the senses at the world, we say, 'it is'. However, the amness of our self and the isness of the world are not two separate beings. They are the same being. There is only one being, infinite being.

This unity of being is the single idea upon which all the great religious and spiritual traditions are founded. It is all we really need to know.

The unity of being is revealed in the experience of beauty. It is never an object, person or landscape that is beautiful. Beauty is an *experience*, not an object. We experience beauty every time the apparent separation between our self and the object, other or world collapses. Beauty is, as such, the dissolution of the subject-object relationship through which we normally perceive the world. In this dissolution, the unity of being is revealed. As Kahlil Gibran said, 'Beauty is eternity gazing at itself in a mirror. But you are eternity and you are the mirror.'* It is the shining of being in everything, as everything.

*   *   *

What is the difference between the being that is your essential nature and the being that is the essential nature of another person or animal?

This is like asking what the difference is between the space in your kitchen and the space in your bedroom. They are the *same* space. The differences belong to the walls within which each space seems to be contained and the objects in each room. But there is no difference in the space itself. Likewise, we all have different thoughts, feelings, perceptions and so on, but there are no differences in our being. The being that shines in each of us as the knowledge 'I am' is the *same* being. When you say, 'I am', and when I say, 'I am', we are referring to the same being.

There are not numerous physical spaces, one for every room. There is *one* vast space of the universe that fills and contains all rooms. Likewise, in reality, there are not numerous beings, one for every person and animal. There is

* *The Prophet*, Kahlil Gibran (Alfred A. Knopf, 1923).

one infinite being that pervades and contains each of us. It is the substance in which we move and live and have our apparently independent existence.

The unity of being is revealed in the experience of love. Ultimately, we do not love a person or an animal. Love is the nature of being. Love does not reside in a person or an animal. Love is the nature of *all* relationships. It may be concealed by conflict, but it is never absent. It is revealed every time the apparent separation between our self and a person or animal dissolves. Love is, as such, the revelation of our shared being.

When we say 'I love you' to someone, we acknowledge that they have the power to dissolve the felt sense of separation between us. In this dissolution, we taste our shared being. *That* is the experience of love. In other words, love is not a relationship between two people, although it may be expressed as such. Love is the dissolution of relationship and the revelation of our prior unity. This is what Rumi meant when he said, 'True friends never really meet; they are in each other all along.'*

The experiences of love and beauty are the revelation of our shared being. When we experience love, we are experiencing the being we share with another person or animal. When we experience beauty, we are experiencing the being we share with an object or nature. Love and beauty are, as such, interventions of reality into our normal, dualistic way of

* My rendition from *The Essential Rumi*, translated by Coleman Barks (Harper-One, 2004).

perceiving the world. Like the white paper of Turner's watercolour painting, they are the shining of being in the landscape of everyday life.

* * *

Imagine that physical space is aware and can think. Now imagine that the space in a room believes it is contained within, limited to and generated by the four walls of the room. If it were to look out the window at the vast space of the universe, it would conceive that space as something other than itself. In other words, it would believe that the vast space of the universe is something that exists outside itself and separate from itself.

The space in the room might then start practising meditation in order to *become* the vast space of the universe. Or, if it was of a religious disposition, it would refer to that vast space as 'God' and seek union with it.

Such is our predicament if we believe that what we essentially are is contained within, limited to and generated by the body. We look at reality through the windows of the senses and see it as a world. We conceive this reality as something that exists outside of and separate from us. Then, we undertake some spiritual practice in order to *become* that reality. Or, if we are of a religious disposition, we name that reality 'God' and seek union with it.

Returning to our analogy of the aware space, imagine that the space in the room meets a friend, another small space.

The friend says, 'Stop looking out of the window; look at *yourself*. See that you are already the vast space of the universe.'

As a result of this encounter, the space turns its gaze around and tastes itself, so to speak. It recognises itself. In that recognition, there is *only* itself, without any limits. It knows itself as the one infinite space of the universe.

Similarly, we are told, 'Turn around and know yourself as you essentially are.' We simply turn around and recognise our being. That is, we know our being again as it essentially is. There is nothing mystical or extraordinary about this. We simply know ourself as we are.

Having recognised its true nature, the space in the room looks out of the window again and sees itself everywhere. Likewise, when we recognise the nature of our being, we look out again through the windows of the senses and see our self everywhere. We know only one infinite being, which shines in us as the amness of our self and in the world as the isness of things.

*   *   *

Whatever I am, I *am*. Whatever the world is, it *is*. Whatever we are, we *are*. Whatever God is, it *is*. Whatever anything is, it *is*. Being is the essence of everyone and everything. As the essence of everyone and everything, being cannot be limited to any particular person or thing. As such, it is unlimited or infinite.

When we look inside, we do not allow our thoughts or feelings to persuade us that we are anything other than infinite
being. We preserve our sacred vision of our self.

When we look outside, we do not allow our perceptions to
persuade us that there are objects, others and a world, as
such. We see through the veneer of separation and otherness
that thought and perception confer on reality. We see
through the apparent multiplicity and diversity of objects
and others to the one infinite reality that lies behind and
manifests as all that we know and experience. We maintain
our sacred vision of the world.

We see the world as William Wordsworth did when he
wrote:

> Thus while the days flew by, and years passed on,
> From Nature and her overflowing soul,
> I had received so much, that all my thoughts
> Were steeped in feeling; I was only then
> Contented, when with bliss ineffable
> I felt the sentiment of Being spread
> O'er all that moves and all that seemeth still;
> O'er all that, lost beyond the reach of thought
> And human knowledge, to the human eye
> Invisible, yet liveth to the heart;
> O'er all that leaps and runs, and shouts and sings,
> Or beats the gladsome air; o'er all that glides
> Beneath the wave, yea, in the wave itself,
> And mighty depth of waters. Wonder not

> If high the transport, great the joy I felt,
> Communing in this sort through earth and heaven
> With every form of creature, as it looked
> Towards the Uncreated with a countenance
> Of adoration, with an eye of love.
> One song they sang, and it was audible,
> Most audible, then, when the fleshly ear,
> O'ercome by humblest prelude of that strain,
> Forgot her functions, and slept undisturbed.*

What is the 'one song' that nature sings? What is the one song of the universe? It is the song of being, nature's anthem. The existence of any object is a hymn of praise to its reality. Everything – every object, all of nature, the entire universe – is singing a continuous hymn of praise to its reality: infinite being, God's being, the only being there is.

* 'The Prelude', Book Two (1850).

CHAPTER 8

ONLY BEING IS

In the presence of the One, all things fade away.
PLOTINUS

Whatever we encounter in the world *exists*. An atom exists, a tree exists, a person exists. Everything in the world exists. Indeed, the entire universe exists.

What is existence? The word 'existence' comes from the Latin prefix *ex*, meaning 'out of' or 'from', and *sistere,* meaning 'to stand', implying that whatever exists 'stands out from' some background or medium. In other words, anything that exists must emerge from, subsist in and disappear into some background or medium.

For example, imagine leaving a bucket of water out on a frosty night. In the morning, you notice that several blocks of ice have formed in the water. The ice has emerged from the water and exists in it. Later that morning, the sun comes out. The ice melts and dissolves back into the water. As such, the water is the substance and reality of the ice, relatively speaking.

Let us relate this to our own experience. In our experience, thoughts emerge, exist and vanish. Feelings arise, exist and dissolve. Objects appear, exist and disappear. The world itself arises, exists and will someday vanish. Out of what background do they arise? In what medium do they temporarily exist and into what will they eventually vanish?

Being.

Being is the reality out of which all existent things arise, in which they exist and into which they vanish when they disappear. It is for this reason that Balyani said, 'When the secret of an atom is discovered, the secret of all created things is made clear.'*

*   *   *

This understanding may be evoked by asking, 'What is but does not exist?'

Anything that exists emerges or 'stands out' from the background of being. Being itself does not exist. If being existed, it would have to emerge or 'stand out' from some background or medium. What would that be? It would have to be prior to being. If it were prior to being, it would not *be*.

Being cannot emerge from non-being. There is nothing prior to being.

Being does not exist; it *is*.

*   *   *

---

* Ibn 'Arabi/Balyani, *op. cit.*

The blocks of ice have a shape, but the water does not. Likewise, everything that exists has a form, be it an atom, a thought, a tree or a world. But being itself is formless.

Everything that exists has a form, and every form can be named. Indeed, language has evolved to name forms. However, being itself cannot legitimately be named. Any name would objectify it and would, as such, render it existent. In other words, it would seem to make an object out of that which has no objective qualities. Even to refer to being as 'being' is not quite right. It is to objectify that which has no objective qualities.

Having no objective qualities, being has no limits. Having no limits in time, it is eternal. Having no limits in space, it is infinite.

The suggestion that being is eternal and infinite does not imply that being is extended indefinitely in all directions of time and space. It implies that being has no dimensions.

Likewise, the suggestion that being is 'here and now' does not mean that it is located at a place in space or a moment in time. It means that being is not *in* the space and time that seem to be known by the mind, just as Turner's moon is not present anywhere in the painting.

Being is formless, nameless and infinite.

*   *   *

When ice forms in the water, nothing new comes into existence. Water simply acquires a temporary name and form, but its essential nature remains the same. When the ice melts, nothing disappears. Water simply loses a temporary name and form. At no point in this process does the essential nature of the water undergo any change.

Likewise, when anything emerges within being, nothing new comes into existence. Being simply acquires a temporary name and form, without ever ceasing to be itself. When anything disappears back into being, nothing is lost. Being simply loses a temporary name and form. At no point in this process does being undergo any change.

As it says in the Bhagavad Gita, 'The unreal never is. The real never ceases to be.'*

Being clothes itself in existence without ever ceasing to be itself.

*   *   *

The ice is not placed into the bucket of water from the outside. It emerges from within the water itself. All there is in the water out of which the ice could be made is the water itself. When the ice forms, nothing is gained.

Likewise, when anything emerges in being – an atom, a person, a tree, a universe – it is not placed into being from

* The Bhagavad Gita 2:16

the outside. Where would it come from? 'Outside of being' would not be. Everything emerges from within being. And all there is in being out of which anything could be made is being itself. Nothing new is created. There is creativity, but no creation!

When the ice melts, it does not leave the water. It just merges back into it. Nothing is lost. Likewise, when anything in existence disappears, it does not leave being. Where would it go? It just dissolves back into being. In fact, even that is not true. It never truly existed, or stood out from being, in the first place. When the object disappears, being simply loses a temporary name and form. There is no destruction.

Being dances as existence; existence rests as being.

*   *   *

All there is to ice is water. There is nothing in the water other than the water out of which the ice could be made. Likewise, all there is to any existent thing is being. There is nothing in being other than being out of which anything could be made.

In other words, nothing real ever comes into existence. Being is continually acquiring and losing temporary names and forms, but there is nothing to those names and forms other than being itself. In Balyani's words, being is 'in each moment in a new configuration'.*

* Ibn 'Arabi/Balyani, *op. cit.*

Nothing exists! There are no things. Only being is.

This is not a depressing, nihilistic statement. It is not a denial of the world. On the contrary, it is a renewal of the world. It is to restore our sacred vision of the world.

Only being is.

CHAPTER 9

THE FIRST AND LAST KNOWLEDGE

I am the Alpha and the Omega,
the First and the Last, the Beginning and the End.
REVELATION 22:13

Other people call you by your name, but you know yourself as 'I'.

These two names reflect two different views of yourself: another person's second-person perspective of you from the outside, and your own first-person, subjective experience* of yourself from within.

When other people refer to you, they call you by the name you were given at birth, such as 'Ruth', 'Joel' or 'Rob'. That is how others refer to you, since they view you from their second-person point of view.

However, 'I' is the name you give to yourself. 'I' is the name *you* give to your own subjective experience of your self from your first-person point of view.

Ruth does not call herself 'Ruth'; she calls herself 'I'. Rob does not call himself 'Rob'; he calls himself 'I'. Likewise, you do not call yourself by your birth name; you call yourself 'I'.

* *Subjective experience* typically refers to one's private, inner experience of thoughts and feelings. However, in this context, it refers to our experience of our essential self, pure being.

'I' is the name that that which knows itself gives to itself. In other words, 'I' is our self's name for itself.

*   *   *

Now, let us consider being.

We refer to Ruth as 'Ruth' because we stand apart from her and view her from a second-person perspective. Likewise, we refer to being as 'being' when we stand apart from it and view it from a second-person perspective. But what about being's own experience of itself?

If being is the ultimate reality of ourself and the world, then being's experience of itself must be the only true view of itself. Any other view of being would be subject to the limitations of the point of view from which it was known. Therefore, only being's subjective experience of itself is absolutely true.

So, what is being's experience of itself?

To know Ruth as 'Ruth', we must stand apart from her as an apparently separate subject of experience. We must view her from a second-person point of view. But being cannot separate itself from itself. It cannot stand apart from itself and view itself from a second-person point of view. That is, it cannot know itself from the outside. Where would it go?

Wherever it went would be 'not being'. If there were a place that was 'not being', that place would not *be*. As Parmenides said, 'Being is; non-being is not.'* In other words, there is no second-person point of view of being; being cannot know itself in subject-object relationship. For this reason, being does not even know itself as 'being'.

Being only knows itself from *its own point of view*. If it could think and speak, being would not call itself 'being'. Being would call itself 'I', for 'I' is the name that that which knows itself gives to itself.

If being were able to describe its experience of itself, it would only say, 'I am'. 'I am' is being's subjective experience of itself. Indeed, 'I am' is being's only experience.

So, even to say 'only being is' or 'there is being' is not quite true. These statements suggest that being is an object of our experience that we know from the point of view of an apparently separate subject. This implies that we are a second being, apart from being. But there are no separate beings other than infinite being who could know being as an object and, thus, name it 'being'.

We have already recognised being as the absolute reality of the universe, so only being's knowledge of itself is absolutely true. Being's knowledge of itself is only 'I am'. Thus, the knowledge 'I am' is the absolute truth.

*   *   *

* Derived from Parmenides's only known work, 'On Nature', which survives only in fragments.

Now, think of God, the absolute, the ultimate.

Just as others must stand apart from you in order to refer to you by your birth name, so we must stand apart from God in order to name God as such.

But God cannot stand apart from itself and know itself from a distance. Where would it go? Wherever it went would be 'not God'. And if there were a place that was 'not God', there would be two realms: 'God' and 'not God'. Then, God would not be infinite and, as such, God would not be God.

Since God cannot stand apart from itself and know itself from a second-person point of view, God does not know itself as 'God'. God can only know itself from *its own point of view*. What is God's knowledge of itself?

'I am'.

It is for this reason that it is truer to say 'I am' than 'God is' or 'being is'.

When we say, 'God is', we subtly deny God. Because to say, 'God is', we must set ourself up as a second being, a temporary, finite being, from whose point of view 'God is'. But God never has the experience 'God is'. God only has the experience 'I am'.

Therefore, to say, 'God is', is to subtly assert the existence of a being apart from God's infinite being, and that is blasphemy. It is for this reason that Meister Eckhart prayed to God to 'rid him of God'.*

* *Selected Writings*, translated by Oliver Davies (Penguin, 1995).

If God *is*, then *only God is*. And if only God is, then only God's knowledge of itself is true knowledge. If God were to express its knowledge of itself, it would not say, 'God is'. It would say, 'I am'.

God's knowledge of itself is pure, unqualified 'I am', without there being any 'God'. Your knowledge of your self is pure, unqualified 'I am', without there being any 'you'.

In other words, the knowledge 'I am' is higher than the knowledge 'God is'. Many who have suggested this were killed by those who believed that the words 'I am' referred to a personal self. But 'I am' refers to the true self, the only self, God's infinite being.

*   *   *

What is the difference between the pure, unqualified 'I am' that is God's knowledge of itself and the pure, unqualified 'I am' that is your knowledge of your self?

Our essential knowledge of our self is 'I am'. In that experience, there is no form. To know our self as a form, we would have to stand apart from our self and view our self from a second-person point of view. But we do not know our self from a second-person point of view. We know our self from our own subjective point of view. Therefore, in our own experience of our self, there is only the experience of formless being. We formulate this by saying, 'I am'.

God's essential knowledge of itself is 'I am'. In that experience, there is no form. To know itself as a form, God would have to stand apart from itself and know itself from a second-person perspective. But God cannot stand apart from itself. It knows itself from its own subjective point of view. Therefore, in God's experience of itself, there is only the experience of formless being. If God could speak, it would formulate this by saying, 'I am'.

The 'I am' is prior to and independent of the content of experience. As such, 'I am' is not coloured or qualified by experience and, therefore, has no limits. It is unlimited or infinite.

Thus, the 'I am' that God is and the 'I am' that you are is the same 'I am'. There is only *one* experience 'I am'.

In its experience of itself, it is just 'I am'. It is not a self, it is not a God, it is not a being. 'I am' is 'I am'.

In other words, our self is not a self. God is not God. Being is not being. There is only 'I am', and 'I am' is only 'I am'.

'I am that I am.'

This is as far as language can go.

* * *

We began our journey by asking, 'What is my primary experience of myself?' And we arrived at the understanding 'I am'. The knowledge 'I am' is our primary experience. It is, as such, the beginning of all knowledge.

Now, we are ending our journey by asking, 'What is being's experience of itself?' And we arrive at the *same* 'I am'. As such, the knowledge 'I am' is the culmination of all knowledge. It is the end of knowledge.

Thus, 'I am' is the origin and the completion of all knowledge. It is the first and last knowledge.

This understanding brings the teaching to an end. It is the essence of Vedanta.* The word 'Vedanta' means 'the end of knowledge'. The essence of Vedanta is not, as such, a body of knowledge. It is not a collection of ideas. It is the end of knowledge, the shining of being, the shining of 'I am'.

You may have been on a spiritual path for several weeks or decades. Sooner or later, we all arrive at the same conclusion: only 'I am' is true; only 'I am' is real.

With this recognition, we step out of our spiritual or religious tradition. We cease being Hindus, Buddhists, Muslims, Jews or Christians, although we may continue to live and practise in the context of our tradition. We step out of our spiritual conditioning – our affiliation with a particular tradition, teacher or teaching – and stand alone as the 'I am', knowing nothing but 'I am'.

Once this understanding is clear, there is no longer a separate self or finite being to practise, progress, become or achieve. There is no one to be ignorant or enlightened.

---

* Vedanta is a Hindu philosophy of non-duality based on the teachings of the Upanishads.

We have undertaken a great journey from the 'I am' that I am to the 'I am' that being is. The place where we start is the place where we end. The entire journey took place in a dream.

There is just the 'I am' that I am.

There is only the shining of being.

When this understanding became clear to me, after exploring these matters for nearly fifty years, there was no elation. I did not become anything that I was not already. I did not achieve or acquire anything.

In fact, a great sorrow arose in me, a sorrow that arose on behalf of humanity. For a while, I felt that I held all of humanity's sorrow in my heart – a sorrow that we should have departed so far from this truth and suffered so terribly as a result. And then an immense silence came over me and I felt, for the first time in my life, that I can now die in peace.

THE ESSENCE OF MEDITATION SERIES

The Essence of Meditation Series presents meditations on the essential, non-dual understanding that lies at the heart of all the great religious and spiritual traditions. Taken from meditations led by Rupert Spira at his meetings and retreats, the simple, contemplative approach presented here encourages a clear seeing of one's experience, leading to an experiential understanding of the peace and causeless joy that are the true nature of our essential being.

Being Aware of Being Aware
The Essence of Meditation Series, Volume I

Being Myself
The Essence of Meditation Series, Volume II

The Heart of Prayer
The Essence of Meditation Series, Volume III

The Shining of Being
The Essence of Meditation Series, Volume IV

From his early teens, Rupert Spira has been deeply interested in the nature of reality and the source of lasting peace and happiness. At seventeen, he learnt to meditate and began a twenty-year period of study and practice in the classical tradition of Advaita Vedanta.

Since then, he has spent several decades studying and practising the philosophies and methods of many of the world's great religious and spiritual traditions, particularly Sufism, Mystical Christianity and the Tantric path of Kashmir Shaivism. Rupert has been distilling the understanding contained in these traditions, through writings, talks and retreats, into a simple approach that leads directly to the recognition of the peace and quiet joy that are our essential nature. Rupert holds regular meetings and retreats in the UK, Europe and the USA, as well as online. He lives in the UK with his wife, Kyra, and has a son, Matthew.

www.rupertspira.com

www.ingramcontent.com/pod-product-compliance
Lightning Source LLC
Chambersburg PA
CBHW030844090426
42737CB00009B/1108